SPOT 50
Dinosaurs

Steve Parker

Miles
KeLLy

First published in 2011 by Miles Kelly Publishing Ltd
Harding's Barn, Bardfield End Green, Thaxted, Essex, CM6 3PX, UK

This edition printed in 2012

2 4 6 8 10 9 7 5 3 1

Publishing Director Belinda Gallagher
Creative Director Jo Cowan
Editor Amanda Askew
Designer Kayleigh Allen
Production Manager Elizabeth Collins
Reprographics Stephan Davis, Jennifer Hunt

ISBN 978-1-84810-599-7

Printed in China

British Library Cataloguing-in-Publication Data
A catalogue record for this book is available from the British Library

ACKNOWLEDGEMENTS
All images are from the Miles Kelly Archives

Made with paper from a sustainable forest

www.mileskelly.net
info@mileskelly.net

www.factsforprojects.com

CONTENTS

Tick the circles when you have spotted the species.

THE AGE OF DINOSAURS

Dinosaurs were a group of prehistoric reptiles that ruled the land for about 150 million years. The Age of Dinosaurs is called the Mesozoic Era. This huge time span is broken down into three smaller chunks of time – the Triassic, Jurassic and Cretaceous periods.

Triassic Period
251–200 mya

The dinosaurs first appeared in the Triassic Period. Fossils of the first-known dinosaurs date back to the mid-Triassic Period about 230 mya. As the period came to an end, the dinosaurs had started to become stronger than their reptile cousins because with an upright stance, they could run faster and further.

Jurassic Period
200–145 mya

During the Jurassic Period, dinosaurs reached their greatest size and spread to the world's major continents. Huge, long-necked herbivores were hunted by fierce, powerful carnivores. The biggest dinosaurs were the sauropods or 'lizard feet'. The Jurassic Period also saw the first bird, *Archaeopteryx*.

Cretaceous Period
145–65 mya

The dinosaurs were at their most varied during the Cretaceous Period. The ornithopods or 'bird feet' quickly became the main plant eaters. The carnivores also became more varied with small, but deadly types such as *Deinonychus*. Thousands of fossils from this period have been discovered.

ANATOMY

Unlike modern reptiles, dinosaurs held their legs directly beneath their bodies. Dinosaurs were closely related to modern crocodiles and it is thought that birds may have evolved from a type of dinosaur.

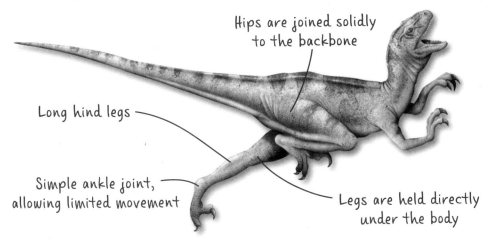

Hips are joined solidly to the backbone

Long hind legs

Simple ankle joint, allowing limited movement

Legs are held directly under the body

Dinosaur groups

Dinosaurs form a large group of reptiles called the Dinosauria. This group is then divided into two smaller groups known as Saurischia (lizard hips) and Ornithischia (bird hips).

Saurischia

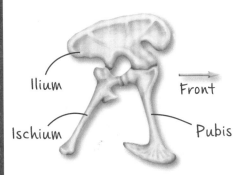

Ilium

Front

Ischium

Pubis

The pubis is angled down and forwards.

Theropods (beast feet)
This group includes meat eaters and some plant eaters. However, nearly all were meat eaters that walked on two legs, with three toes on each foot.

Sauropods (lizard feet)
All these dinosaurs were plant eaters, with long necks, bulky bodies, long tails and pillar-like legs.

Ornithischia

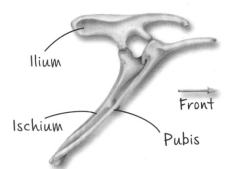

Ilium

Front

Ischium

Pubis

The pubis is angled down and backwards.

This group was only plant eaters.

Ornithopods (bird feet)

Stegosaurs (roofed or plated lizards)

Ankylosaurs (armoured lizards)

Pachycephalosaurs (bone heads)

Ceratopsians (horn faces)

COELOPHYSIS

The hollow bones and slim build of *Coelophysis* would have made it extremely light. Its sharp teeth were probably used for grabbing small prey such as lizards and worms. *Coelophysis* was probably the fastest land dinosaur of the Triassic Period and maybe the fastest of all animals of the time, with an estimated top speed of 40 km/h. Remains of many hundreds of individuals have been found at a site called Ghost Ranch in New Mexico, USA.

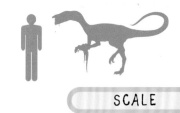

SCALE

In 1998, the space shuttle took a skull of Coelophysis into space, where it was taken on board the Mir space station.

FACT FILE

Latin name *Coelophysis bauri*
Pronounced see-low-FI-sis
Group Theropod
Diet Carnivore
When it lived 220 mya

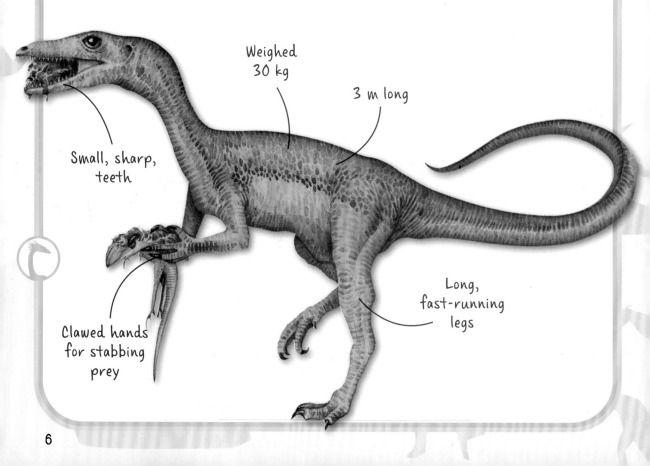

Weighed 30 kg

3 m long

Small, sharp, teeth

Clawed hands for stabbing prey

Long, fast-running legs

HERRERASAURUS

A powerful predator, *Herrerasaurus* was named after Argentinian goat-herder, **Victorino Herrera, who discovered its fossils.** It is one of several very early dinosaurs from the Middle to Late Triassic Period found in what is now South America. *Herrerasaurus* had long, narrow jaws filled with sharp, back-curving teeth, and strong rear legs allowing it to move quickly. It probably hunted small animals such as lizards, insects and other reptiles.

SCALE

Able to move at speed, Herrerasaurus may be the oldest meat-eating dinosaur ever discovered.

FACT FILE

Latin name
Herrerasaurus ischigualastensis

Pronounced
huh-RARE-uh-SAW-rus

Group Theropod

Diet Carnivore

When it lived 225 mya

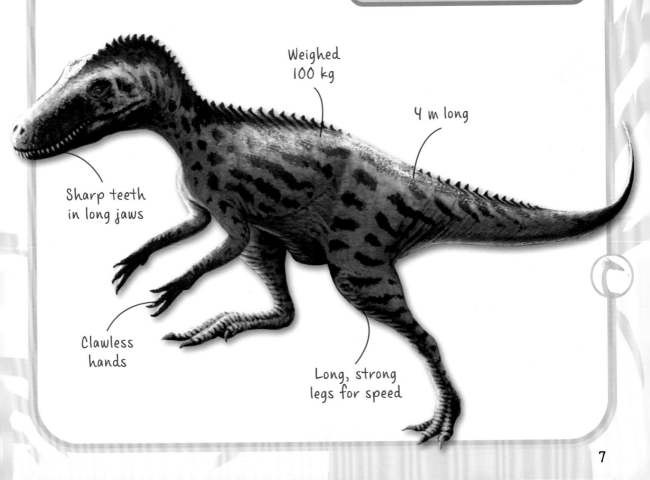

Weighed 100 kg

4 m long

Sharp teeth in long jaws

Clawless hands

Long, strong legs for speed

PLATEOSAURUS

One of the first large dinosaurs, *Plateosaurus* is well known from many skeletons. The bones were unearthed at various sites in Europe, including France, Switzerland and Germany. Its long body, sturdy hips and powerful, weighty tail could mean that it reared up on its hind limbs and leaned back, using its muscular tail for support. In this way it could reach tree ferns and other plant food 5 m above the ground.

SCALE

FACT FILE

Latin name
Plateosaurus engelhardti
Pronounced plate-e-o-SAW-rus
Group Sauropod
Diet Herbivore
When it lived 210 mya

The thumbs of Plateosaurus ended in a large spike that was used for jabbing at enemies and grasping food.

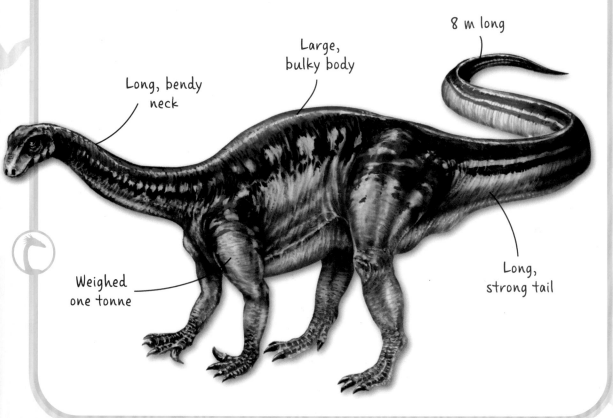

Large, bulky body

8 m long

Long, bendy neck

Long, strong tail

Weighed one tonne

PROCOMPSOGNATHUS

A meat eater, *Procompsognathus* was **lightweight and agile.** Its teeth were more suited to hunting live prey, such as newly hatched dinosaurs, rather than for scavenging. Its tail formed almost half of its total length, and instead of being whip-like, it was probably quite stiff. The name '*Pro* (before) *Compsognathus*' is true in that the smaller *Compsognathus* lived later, and the two dinosaurs were similar in shape. However, more than 60 million years separated these dinosaurs.

Procompsognathus was about the same weight as a domestic cat — but it was much slimmer and twice as long.

FACT FILE

Latin name
Procompsognathus triassicus
Pronounced
pro-comp-sog-NATH-us
Group Theropod
Diet Carnivore
When it lived 215 mya

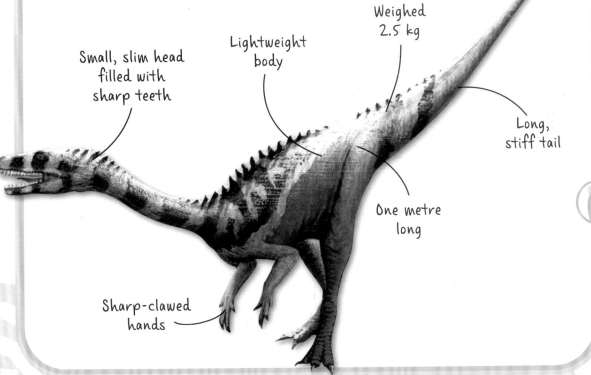

Weighed 2.5 kg

Lightweight body

Small, slim head filled with sharp teeth

Long, stiff tail

One metre long

Sharp-clawed hands

RIOJASAURUS

The remains of *Riojasaurus*, one of the first truly large dinosaurs, date back to 220 mya. They were first discovered in the 1920s in the La Rioja district of Argentina; hence the name. Further fossils have since been found of more than 20 individuals. *Riojasaurus* probably moved on all fours but perhaps reared up on its back legs, like *Plateosaurus*, to reach leaves several metres off the ground.

SCALE

Riojasaurus did not chew its food. It swallowed stones to help grind up the food in its huge stomach.

FACT FILE

Latin name
Riojasaurus incertis
Pronounced ree-O-ha-SAW-rus
Group Sauropod
Diet Herbivore
When it lived 215 mya

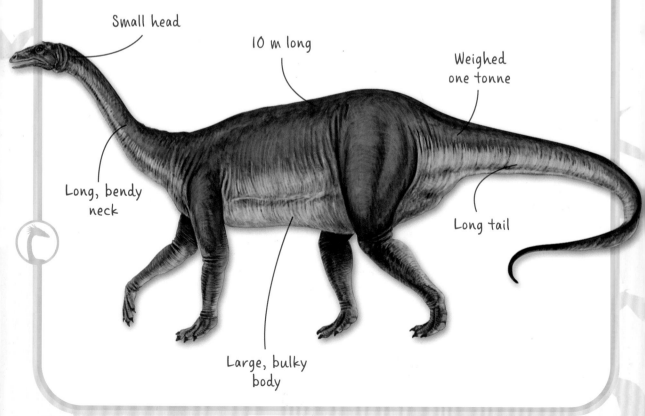

Small head

10 m long

Weighed one tonne

Long, bendy neck

Long tail

Large, bulky body

SYNTARSUS

This fast-moving dinosaur was one of the first meat eaters of the Triassic Period. It was a swift runner and was able to grab and hold down its prey with its long, sharp-clawed hands. Its jaws were filled with lots of sharp teeth. The bones of several *Syntarsus* have been found in Zimbabwe, Africa, and this suggests that the dinosaur may have lived in herds. The four-toed feet were joined at the ankle, giving the dinosaur its name.

SCALE

The head crest of Syntarsus has been found on fossils from North America, but it is missing from those found in Africa.

FACT FILE

Latin name
Syntarsus rhodesiensis
Pronounced sin-TAR-sus
Group Theropod
Diet Carnivore
When it lived 200 mya

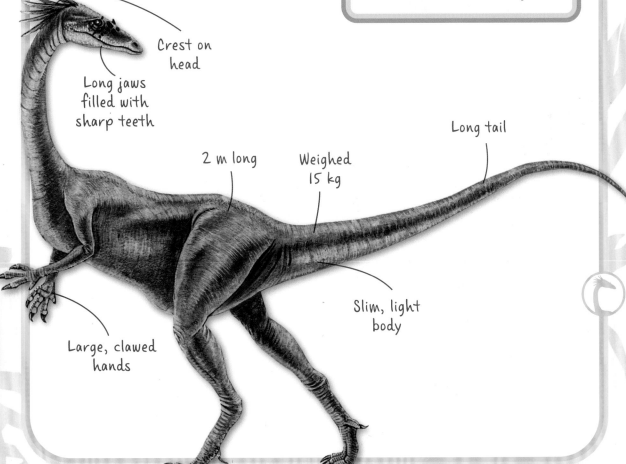

Crest on head

Long jaws filled with sharp teeth

Long tail

2 m long

Weighed 15 kg

Slim, light body

Large, clawed hands

ALLOSAURUS

The largest meat eater of the Late Jurassic Period, *Allosaurus* would have rivalled *Tyrannosaurus rex* in size. This fierce hunter preyed on giant dinosaurs such as *Diplodocus*. Most *Allosaurus* fossils have been found in the American Midwest, including the remains of more than 65 animals in the Cleveland-Lloyd Dinosaur Quarry, Utah, USA. However, fossils have also been identified in Africa and a 'dwarf' version has been found in Australia and Europe.

SCALE

The huge teeth of Allosaurus curved backwards to prevent its struggling prey from escaping its massive jaws.

FACT FILE

Latin name *Allosaurus fragilis*
Pronounced aL-o-SAW-rus
Group Theropod
Diet Carnivore
When it lived 150 mya

Powerful jaws with long teeth

Long tail

Weighed 2 tonnes

12 m long

Sharp, clawed hands

Long, strong legs and clawed feet

APATOSAURUS

The first fossils of *Apatosaurus* were found in 1877. However in 1879, similar remains were discovered and named *Brontosaurus*. Many years later, it was agreed that both sets of fossils were the same dinosaur, and so the name *Brontosaurus* was dropped. Despite its huge size, *Apatosaurus* could move surprisingly quickly. A sharp, 17-cm-long claw on each front foot may have helped it to balance.

SCALE

The head of Apatosaurus was tiny, compared to its huge body – hardly bigger than the head of a modern-day pony.

FACT FILE

Latin name *Apatosaurus ajax*
Pronounced ah-PAT-o-SAW-rus
Group Sauropod
Diet Herbivore
When it lived 152 mya

Tiny head with peg-like teeth

23 m long

Weighed 30 tonnes

82 bones in the tail – used as a whip against enemies

Massive, pillar-like legs

BAROSAURUS

Compared to its long neck and tail, *Barosaurus* had a relatively small body. Its amazingly long neck had 16 to 17 vertebrae, or neck bones, some almost one metre in length. This would have allowed *Barosaurus* to reach the highest branches, needles and leaves of towering tree ferns, gingkoes and conifers. Remains of this long-necked herbivore have been identified at sites in Utah and South Dakota, USA, and possibly in Tanzania, east Africa.

SCALE

Despite its huge size, Barosaurus may have been able to rear up onto its back legs to feed from the tallest trees.

FACT FILE

Latin name *Barosaurus lentus*
Pronounced bare-o-SAW-rus
Group Sauropod
Diet Herbivore
When it lived 155 mya

Long neck for reaching the highest leaves

25 m long

Weighed 30 tonnes

Relatively small body with long tail

Big, bulky legs

BRACHIOSAURUS

One of the most widespread dinosaurs, remains of *Brachiosaurus* have been found in Africa, Europe and North America. *Brachiosaurus* is still the biggest dinosaur known from fairly complete fossil remains. Its name means Arm Reptile, which refers to its long front legs. Along with its flagpole-length neck, these allowed *Brachiosaurus* to reach food 14 m above the ground. There seems to be no reason for the position of its nostrils – rather than at the front of its snout, they were on top of its arched head.

SCALE

Brachiosaurus had similar body proportions to a giraffe, but was more than twice as tall and 50 times heavier.

FACT FILE

Latin name
Brachiosaurus altithorax
Pronounced brack-ee-o-SAW-rus
Group Sauropod
Diet Herbivore
When it lived 150 mya

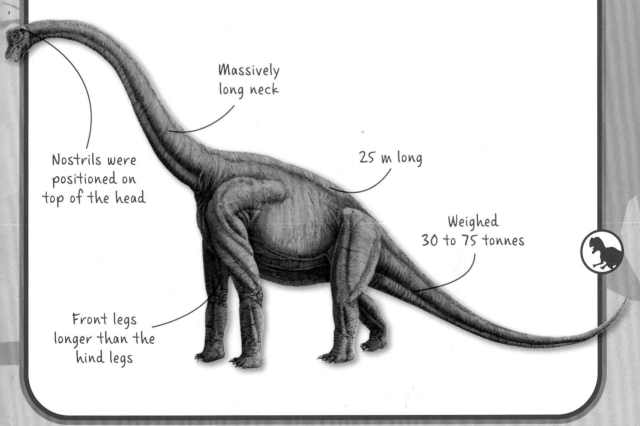

Massively long neck

25 m long

Weighed 30 to 75 tonnes

Nostrils were positioned on top of the head

Front legs longer than the hind legs

CAMARASAURUS

The neck and tail of *Camarasaurus* were shorter and thicker than many of its cousins such as *Brachiosaurus* and *Diplodocus*. It is one of the best known of all the big dinosaurs because so many almost complete fossil skeletons have been found. The skeleton of a young *Camarasaurus* was uncovered in the 1920s, and had nearly every bone in its body lying in the correct position as they were in life – an amazingly rare find.

SCALE

The name 'Camarasaurus' means 'Chambered Reptile' because the bones in its back and neck were hollow.

FACT FILE

Latin name
Camarasaurus supremus
Pronounced
kam-uh-ruh-SAW-rus
Group Sauropod
Diet Herbivore
When it lived 152 mya

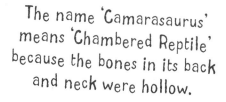

Small head

Short, thick neck

Powerful, bulky body

20 m long

Weighed 20 tonnes

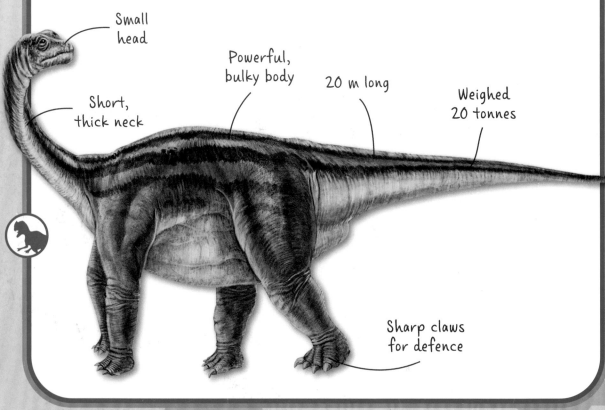

Sharp claws for defence

CERATOSAURUS

A fierce hunter, *Ceratosaurus* lived at the same time and in the same place as its bigger cousin, *Allosaurus*. It could run quickly and its big jaws were filled with sharp, fang-like teeth. The horn on its nose was probably too small to be used as a weapon, but it may have been a sign of a mature adult. This dinosaur had bony lumps above its eyes.

SCALE

Ceratosaurus had four-fingered hands. This was a very primitive feature, as most Jurassic meat eaters had only three fingers.

FACT FILE

Latin name
Ceratosaurus nasicornus
Pronounced sir-RAT-oh-saw-rus
Group Theropod
Diet Carnivore
When it lived 150 mya

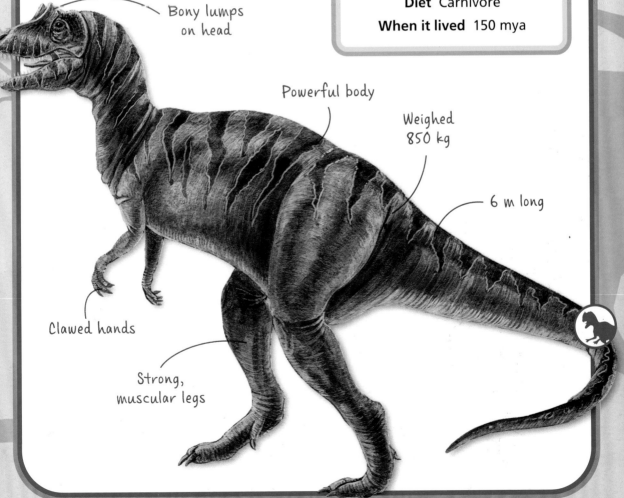

Bony lumps
on head

Powerful body

Weighed
850 kg

6 m long

Clawed hands

Strong,
muscular legs

COMPSOGNATHUS

The smallest dinosaur, *Compsognathus* is known from fairly complete fossils. Not much larger than a pet cat, it weighed just 2 kg. Its back legs were hardly thicker than a human thumb, the front legs were pencil-slim, and half of its length was made up of a whip-like tail. However, this little dinosaur was a fierce predator of small prey such as insects, worms, lizards, and perhaps newly hatched dinosaurs.

SCALE

Compsognathus may have been related to Archaeopteryx, the first bird, as its fossils are from the same time and region.

FACT FILE

Latin name
Compsognathus longipes
Pronounced komp-sog-NATH-us
Group Theropod
Diet Carnivore
When it lived 150 mya

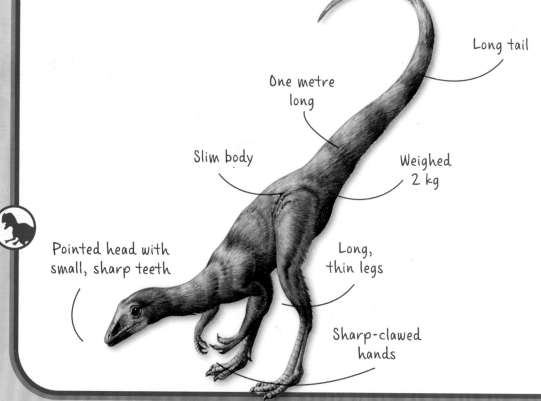

Long tail

One metre long

Slim body

Weighed 2 kg

Pointed head with small, sharp teeth

Long, thin legs

Sharp-clawed hands

DILOPHOSAURUS

One of the biggest early meat-eating dinosaurs, *Dilophosaurus* was a fast, agile hunter. It had sharp, curved teeth, easily able to run down prey such as the newly hatched young of large herbivores. Its name means 'Two-ridged Reptile' after its head crest – two narrow, curved plates of bone projecting from the forehead. This crest may have been used to attract a mate, or to help distinguish males from females.

SCALE

Dilophosaurus was about the same weight as the biggest polar bears of today – and probably just as fierce.

FACT FILE

Latin name
Dilophosaurus wetherilli

Pronounced
die-LOAF-o-SAW-rus

Group Theropod

Diet Carnivore

When it lived 200 mya

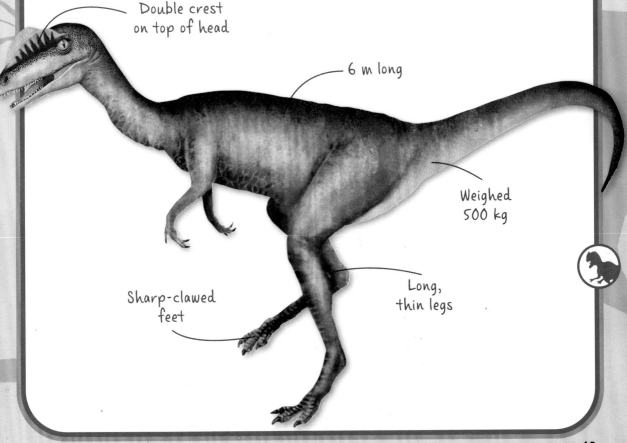

Double crest on top of head

6 m long

Weighed 500 kg

Sharp-clawed feet

Long, thin legs

EUSTREPTOSPONDYLUS

In the Middle Jurassic Period this fierce predator roamed near what is now Oxford, southern England. Much larger than its equivalent carnivores of today, the big cats, *Eustreptospondylus* ran quickly on its strong back legs and four-toed feet, although only three toes touched the ground. Its large head contained long jaws filled with sharp, saw-edged teeth. *Eustreptospondylus* may have hunted stegosaurs and sauropods, as both groups roamed the same region at the time.

SCALE

When first discovered, scientists thought that Eustreptospondylus was actually the remains of Megalosaurus.

FACT FILE

Latin name
Eustreptospondylus oxoniensis

Pronounced
u-STREP-toe-spon-DI-lus

Group Theropod

Diet Carnivore

When it lived 160 mya

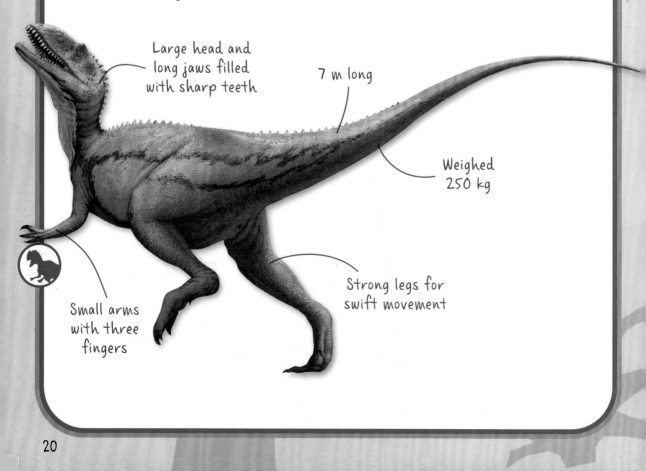

Large head and long jaws filled with sharp teeth

7 m long

Weighed 250 kg

Strong legs for swift movement

Small arms with three fingers

JANENSCHIA

This huge herbivore was named after Werner Janensch, a German palaeontologist who discovered its remains. It walked on four thick, pillar-like legs and its rear feet may have had claws. Like other large herbivore dinosaurs, *Janenschia* probably had a very powerful heart to pump blood around its enormous body. Only a few leg fossils of *Janenschia* have been found – one thigh bone alone was 1.4 m long.

SCALE

There is a possibility that Janenschia may have been covered in bony plates for protection.

FACT FILE

Latin name *Janenschia robusta*
Pronounced jay-NEN-she-uh
Group Sauropod
Diet Herbivore
When it lived 156 mya

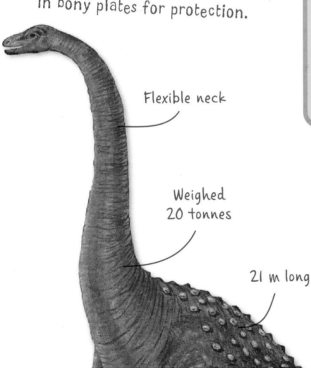

Flexible neck

Weighed 20 tonnes

21 m long

Long tail

KENTROSAURUS

Like other members of the stegosaur group, *Kentrosaurus* had a double row of long, bony plates and spikes for protection. It had a beak-shaped mouth for nipping plants and an arched back. The tiny head held a tiny brain – this dinosaur wasn't very intelligent. It moved slowly, eating low-lying plants most of the time.

SCALE

Some of the best fossils of Kentrosaurus were destroyed in the bombing raids on Germany during World War II.

FACT FILE

Latin name
Kentrosaurus longispinus
Pronounced ken-TROH-saw-rus
Group Stegosaur
Diet Herbivore
When it lived 155 mya

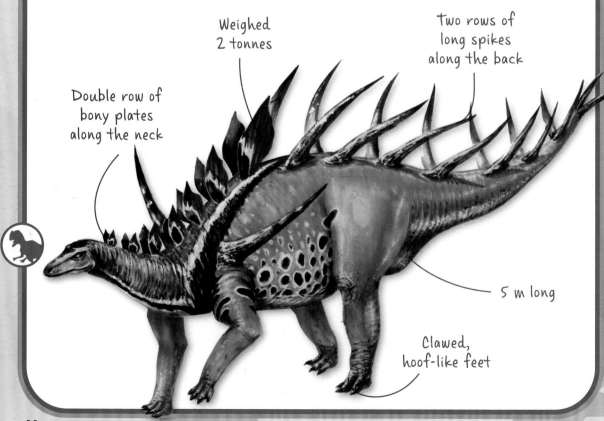

Weighed
2 tonnes

Two rows of
long spikes
along the back

Double row of
bony plates
along the neck

5 m long

Clawed,
hoof-like feet

MEGALOSAURUS

This dinosaur was a large meat eater. It had small front arms and a huge skull. Its long, stiff tail was kept off the ground, and *Megalosaurus* was able to run at speed over short distances. The sharp teeth were curved, with a saw-toothed edge. It had inward-pointing toes, and strong sharp claws on both feet and hands. When *Megalosaurus* was discovered in 1822, the word 'dinosaur' did not even exist. It was not until 1841 that dinosaurs were recognized as a new group of extinct reptiles.

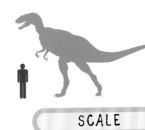

SCALE

Early scientists thought that Megalosaurus walked on four legs like other reptiles – today we know it walked on two.

FACT FILE

Latin name
Megalosaurus bucklandii

Pronounced
MEG-ah-low-saw-rus

Group Theropod

Diet Carnivore

When it lived 160 mya

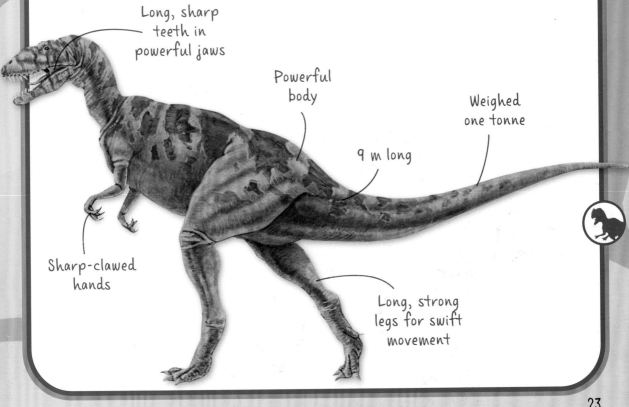

Long, sharp teeth in powerful jaws

Powerful body

9 m long

Weighed one tonne

Sharp-clawed hands

Long, strong legs for swift movement

ORNITHOLESTES

This lightweight, meat-eating dinosaur was once believed to have chased and eaten early types of birds, such as *Archaeopteryx*. This fact is now in debate as the fossils of these two creatures, both from the Late Jurassic Period, were found thousands of kilometres apart. The long, powerful arms and hands had curved claws like bent daggers – ideal for catching small prey. The rear legs were also long and slim, but very powerful, allowing *Ornitholestes* to run fast. Only one fossilized skeleton has been discovered.

SCALE

FACT FILE

Latin name
Ornitholestes hermanni

Pronounced
or-ni-thoe-LESS-tees

Group Theropod

Diet Carnivore

When it lived 144 mya

Ornitholestes had exceptionally long fingers – ideal for grabbing baby dinosaurs newly hatched from their eggs.

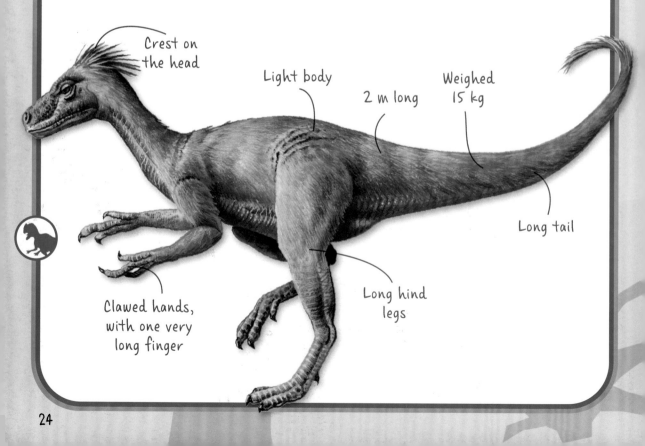

Crest on the head

Light body

2 m long

Weighed 15 kg

Long tail

Clawed hands, with one very long finger

Long hind legs

SHUNOSAURUS

A smaller sauropod, *Shunosaurus* had a shorter neck, but still had the bulky body and long tail of its group. Its most noticeable feature was a tail club made of enlarged bones, possibly armed with several spikes. This would be an effective defensive weapon when swung at attacking carnivores. Remains of *Shunosaurus* include five skulls, which is unusual as the skull is among the smallest, most fragile part of a sauropod's body and rarely fossilizes.

SCALE

Shunosaurus may have lived to be more than 100 years of age. It is the only sauropod dinosaur to have a spiked tail.

FACT FILE

Latin name *Shunosaurus lii*
Pronounced shoo-no-SAW-rus
Group Sauropod
Diet Herbivore
When it lived 170 mya

Spiked tail used for defence

Big, bulky body

11 m long

Weighed 10 tonnes

Short legs

STEGOSAURUS

One of the puzzles about dinosaurs is the reason for the tall, diamond-shaped back plates of *Stegosaurus*. They were made of lightweight bone, probably covered by skin, and were of little use for protection. Perhaps they worked as heat absorbers to soak up the sun's warmth so that this herbivore could get moving more quickly in the morning than other cold-blooded dinosaurs. *Stegosaurus* had a spiked tail that it used to swing at enemies.

SCALE

Stegosaurus is thought to have had the smallest brain for its body size of all the dinosaurs – about the size of a golf ball.

FACT FILE

Latin name
Stegosaurus armatus
Pronounced steg-o-SAW-rus
Group Stegosaur
Diet Herbivore
When it lived 155 mya

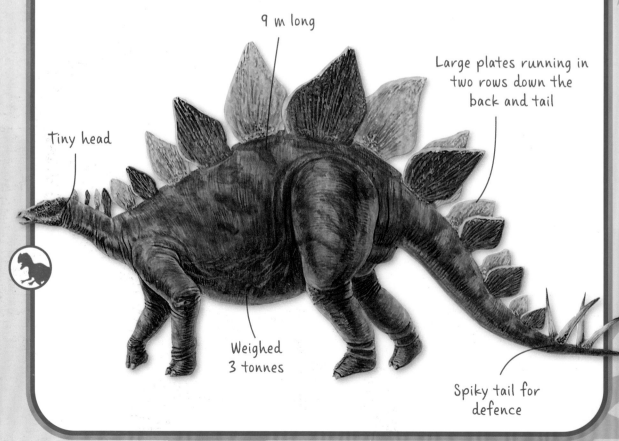

9 m long

Large plates running in two rows down the back and tail

Tiny head

Weighed 3 tonnes

Spiky tail for defence

TUOJIANGOSAURUS

Named after the Tuo River in China, this plant eater showed how the stegosaurs had spread to most continents by the Late Jurassic Period. Like other stegosaurs, *Tuojiangosaurus* had tall triangular plates of bone along its back. These probably stuck upright in two rows. The bird-like beak cropped low vegetation, and the four large spikes at the end of the tail were arranged as two V-shapes in a formidable defensive weapon.

SCALE

The plates on the back of *Tuojiangosaurus* were probably used to stop its body temperature getting too hot.

FACT FILE

Latin name
Tuojiangosaurus multispinus
Pronounced
two-oh-jee-ang-oh-SAW-rus
Group Stegosaur
Diet Herbivore
When it lived 150 mya

Four-spiked tail

Double row of bony plates

7 m long

Small head with beak-shaped mouth

Weighed one tonne

ANKYLOSAURUS

This dinosaur was covered in thick, bony plates for defence. However, it had a soft, unprotected belly – which meant it walked close to the ground. *Ankylosaurus* had a powerful tail club made up of plates of bone that could be swung with great force, like a hammer. This tail club was nearly one metre across and could deliver a crippling blow to an enemy.

SCALE

Ankylosaurus weighed as much as a modern-day elephant. The huge club at the end of its tail weighed 50 kg alone.

FACT FILE

Latin name
Ankylosaurus magniventris
Pronounced an-KIE-low-saw-rus
Group Ankylosaur
Diet Herbivore
When it lived 70 mya

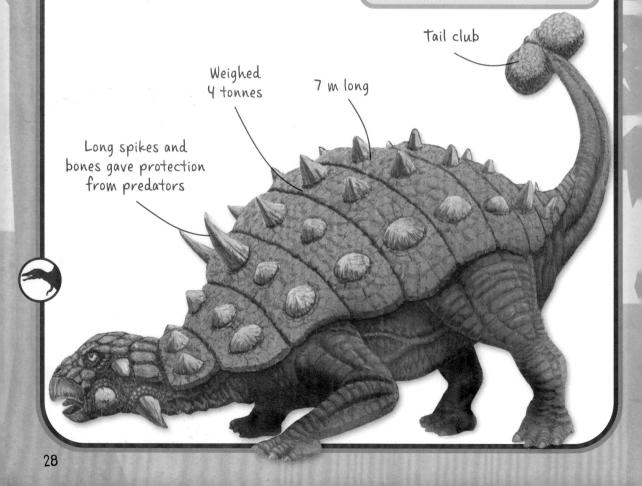

Tail club

Weighed
4 tonnes

7 m long

Long spikes and bones gave protection from predators

AVIMIMUS

This small dinosaur lived mainly in what is now the Gobi Desert in Mongolia. Its strong, sharp beak pecked for its food of small animals and perhaps plants. Some clues in its fossilized bones suggest that *Avimimus* had feathers, at least on its forearms. However, the arms were too small and weak for flight, so the feathers may have been for warmth or camouflage.

SCALE

Some experts believe there are strong links between Avimimus and birds — both have feathers, toothless beaks and slim necks.

FACT FILE

Latin name
Avimimus portentosus
Pronounced AY-vee-MIM-us
Group Theropod
Diet Omnivore
When it lived 95 mya

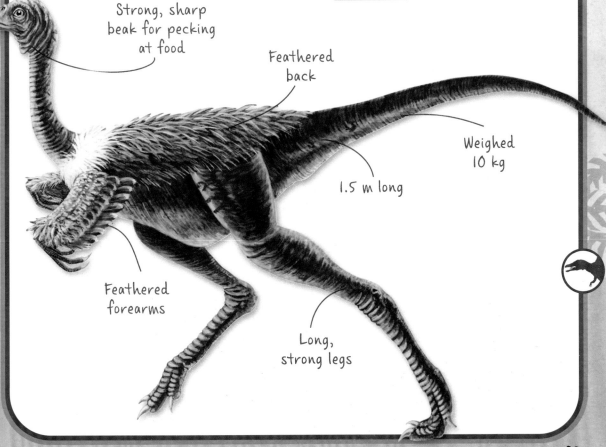

Strong, sharp beak for pecking at food

Feathered back

Weighed 10 kg

1.5 m long

Feathered forearms

Long, strong legs

BARYONYX

Long, lean and swift, *Baryonyx* was named for the huge curving claw on each hand. It may have been a fish hunter, wading in rivers and streams to stab its prey with its clawed hands. Its jaws were long and slim, like those of a crocodile.

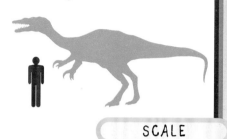

SCALE

Baryonyx may have had more than 100 sharp, saw–like teeth. This is more than most other theropod dinosaurs.

FACT FILE

Latin name *Baryonyx walkeri*
Pronounced bare-ee-ON-ix
Group Theropod
Diet Carnivore
When it lived 125 mya

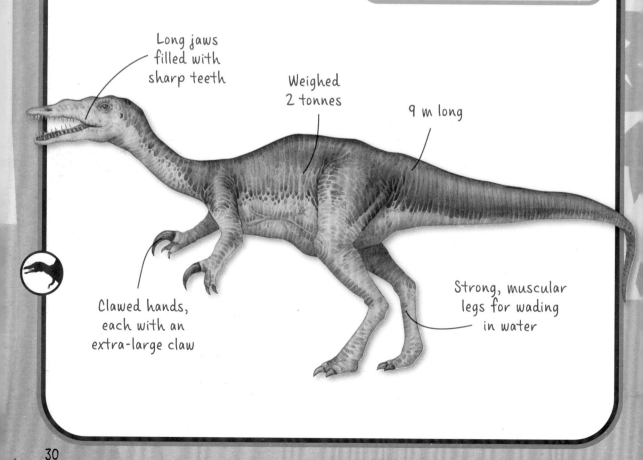

Long jaws filled with sharp teeth

Weighed 2 tonnes

9 m long

Clawed hands, each with an extra-large claw

Strong, muscular legs for wading in water

CAUDIPTERYX

This dinosaur had various bird features. *Caudipteryx* had a beak, with teeth in the upper jaw, feathers on its body and front limbs, and a long, feathered tail. The front limbs were not used for flying, suggesting that the feathers were for warmth (it may have been warm-blooded) or for colourful displays to attract a mate at breeding time. *Caudipteryx* was about the size of a modern-day turkey.

SCALE

Fossil remains of Caudipteryx indicate that it probably swallowed small stones to help it digest its food.

FACT FILE

Latin name *Caudipteryx zoui*
Pronounced cow-DIP-tuh-riks
Group Theropod
Diet Omnivore
When it lived 140 mya

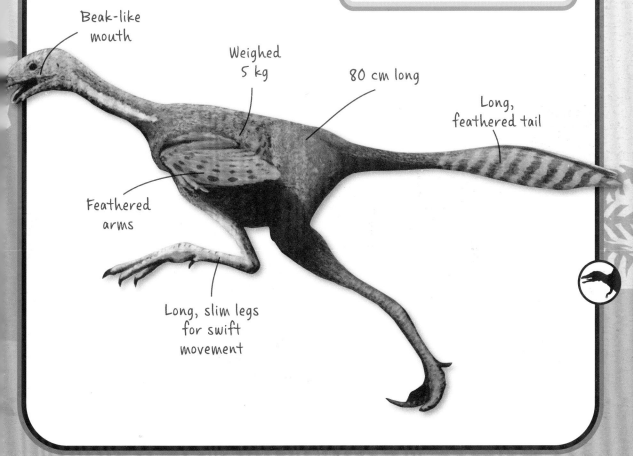

Beak-like mouth

Weighed 5 kg

80 cm long

Long, feathered tail

Feathered arms

Long, slim legs for swift movement

CORYTHOSAURUS

This dinosaur was a hadrosaur – a large 'duckbilled' creature with a bony crest on its head. Its name means 'Corinthian Helmet Reptile', which refers to this crest, which resembled the helmets of soldiers from Corinth, ancient Greece. Hadrosaurs had strong back legs and quite large front legs. They could probably run along on all fours or rear up on their hind legs to feed. Fossil skin of *Corythosaurus* has also been found – it had a strange pebbly texture.

SCALE

FACT FILE

Latin name
Corythosaurus casuarius

Pronounced
core-ITH-oh-SAW-rus

Group Ornithopod

Diet Herbivore

When it lived 75 mya

The crest of Corythosaurus was probably connected to its nose. This may have allowed it to make noises like an elephant.

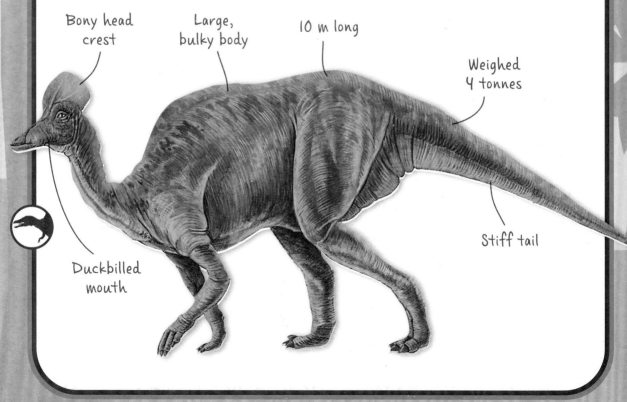

Bony head crest

Large, bulky body

10 m long

Weighed 4 tonnes

Stiff tail

Duckbilled mouth

DEINONYCHUS

A strong predator, *Deinonychus* was named after the sharp, curving claw on the second toe of each foot. The joints in the toe allowed the claw to be held off the ground when walking or running, to keep it sharp. It could be swung in a fast, slashing motion to attack victims. *Deinonychus* fossils have been found in groups, suggesting that this dinosaur was a pack hunter. Some scientists think that *Deinonychus* could leap onto its prey to attack it.

SCALE

Deinonychus was one of the most intelligent dinosaurs. It probably hunted in packs, in planned attacks.

FACT FILE

Latin name
Deinonychus antirrhopus
Pronounced die-NON-ee-kuss
Group Theropod
Diet Carnivore
When it lived 120 mya

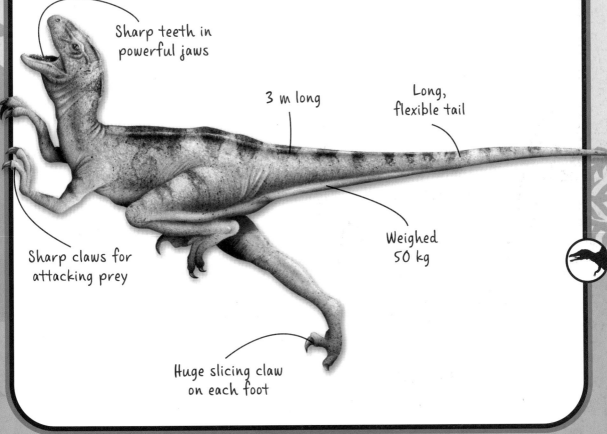

Sharp teeth in powerful jaws

3 m long

Long, flexible tail

Sharp claws for attacking prey

Weighed 50 kg

Huge slicing claw on each foot

EDMONTONIA

This heavy dinosaur was covered in bony lumps and plates that acted like a suit of armour. It probably charged and jabbed predators with its neck and shoulder spikes. The beak-like mouth was filled with small teeth. *Edmontonia* probably chewed its food at length and may have kept food in pouches in its mouth. The earliest remains of *Edmontonia* were discovered in 1924 in Canada. The rock layers in which the dinosaur was found are called the Edmonton Formation, and gave this dinosaur its name.

SCALE

FACT FILE

Latin name
Edmontonia longiceps
Pronounced ed-mon-TOE-nee-uh
Group Ankylosaur
Diet Herbivore
When it lived 75 mya

The body of Edmontonia was so well protected, it even had bony armour covering its eyelids.

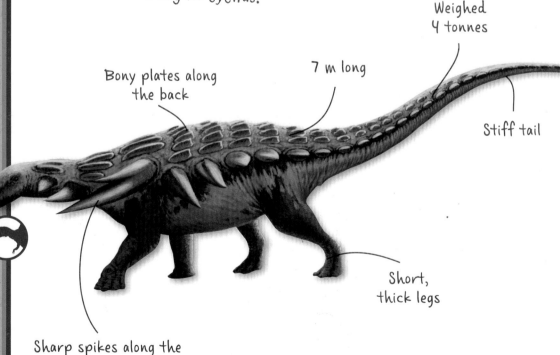

Weighed 4 tonnes

7 m long

Bony plates along the back

Stiff tail

Short, thick legs

Sharp spikes along the shoulders and neck

GIGANOTOSAURUS

For almost 100 years, *Tyrannosaurus rex* held the record for being the largest meat eater ever to walk the Earth. This changed in 1994 when fossils of an even greater carnivore were discovered in the Patagonia region of Argentina. Named *Giganotosaurus*, this theropod was huge, and its teeth were more than 20 cm in length. *Giganotosaurus* preyed on the massive sauropod dinosaurs.

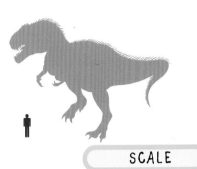

SCALE

FACT FILE

Latin name
Giganotosaurus carolinii

Pronounced
jig-an-o-toe-SAW-rus

Group Theropod

Diet Carnivore

When it lived 100 mya

The head of Giganotosaurus measured 1.8 m – as long as an adult person is tall. Its body was as long as a bus.

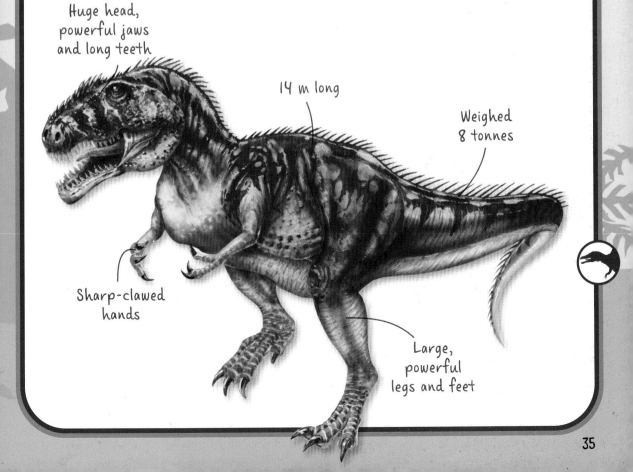

Huge head, powerful jaws and long teeth

14 m long

Weighed 8 tonnes

Sharp-clawed hands

Large, powerful legs and feet

HYPSILOPHODON

This small, fast plant eater may have lived in herds like modern-day antelopes. It had a long, straight tail to help it balance and strong, sturdy claws that it probably used to scrabble and dig in soil for seeds and roots. Several fossils of *Hypsilophodon* have been found together, which may mean that a whole group or herd probably died in a flood, or trying to cross a river.

SCALE

Early dinosaur experts thought that Hypsilophodon might have lived in trees – a theory that has now been proved as untrue.

FACT FILE

Latin name
Hypsilophodon foxii

Pronounced
hip-sih-LOFF-oh-don

Group Ornithopod

Diet Herbivore

When it lived 125 mya

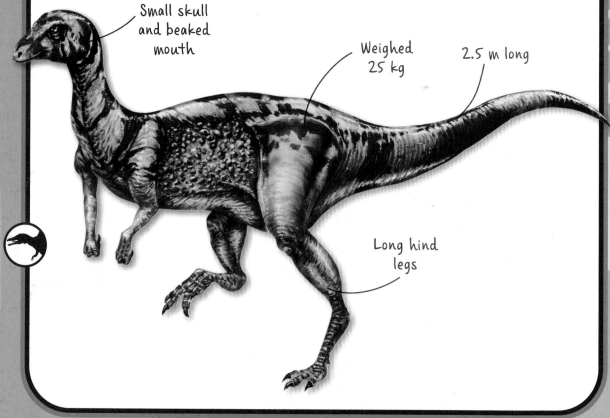

Small skull and beaked mouth

Weighed 25 kg

2.5 m long

Long hind legs

IGUANODON

One of the best-studied dinosaurs, many fossils of *Iguanodon* have been found. At one coal mine in Belgium, the remains of about 40 almost complete skeletons jumbled together were found. This suggests that a herd died, perhaps while trying to cross a river. On each 'thumb' (first front toe), *Iguanodon* had a sharp spike for jabbing at enemies. This dinosaur weighed about the same as an African elephant.

SCALE

In early reconstructions, the spike of Iguanodon was placed on its nose, as scientists didn't realize it was part of its hand.

FACT FILE

Latin name
Iguanodon bernissartensis
Pronounced ig-WHA-no-don
Group Ornithopod
Diet Herbivore
When it lived 130 mya

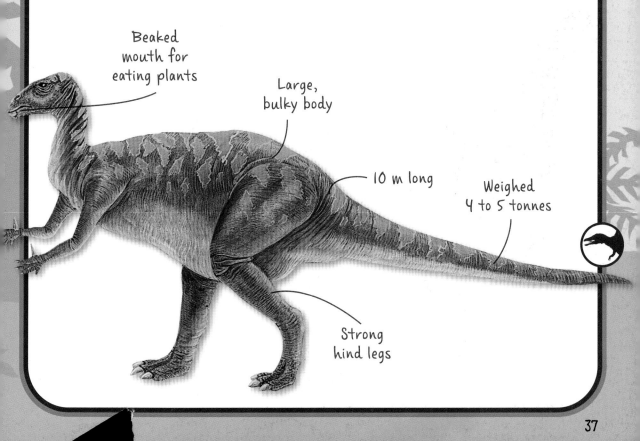

Beaked
mouth for
eating plants

Large,
bulky body

10 m long

Weighed
4 to 5 tonnes

Strong
hind legs

JOBARIA

A huge sauropod from the Early Cretaceous Period, *Jobaria* had a relatively short neck and spoon-like teeth. It may have been able to rear up onto its hind legs for feeding or in defence. A near complete skeleton of this herbivore was found in 1997 in Niger, Africa. *Jobaria* was named after Jobar, a mythical creature of the Tuareg people from North Africa.

SCALE

When Jobaria was alive, 135 mya, the Sahara desert would have been covered with trees and lakes.

FACT FILE

Latin name *Jobaria tiguidensis*
Pronounced jo-BAH-ria
Group Sauropod
Diet Herbivore
When it lived 135 mya

Tiny head

Extremely long neck for grazing from the tallest trees

20 m long

Weighed 25 tonnes

Huge, thick legs

LAMBEOSAURUS

This dinosaur had a wide, flat, toothless mouth that was similar to a duck's beak. *Lambeosaurus* gathered plants that were then crushed to a pulp by rows of sharp-ridged cheek teeth. A hollow head crest projected at a right angle from its head, which may have identified males from females, or may even have been used to call to each other during the mating season. This dinosaur was named after Lawrence Lambe, an early Canadian fossil hunter.

SCALE

Lambeosaurus weighed more than an elephant, but could run slowly for several hours. It is the largest duckbilled dinosaur.

FACT FILE

Latin name
Lambeosaurus lambei
Pronounced lam-bee-o-SAW-rus
Group Ornithopod
Diet Herbivore
When it lived 77 mya

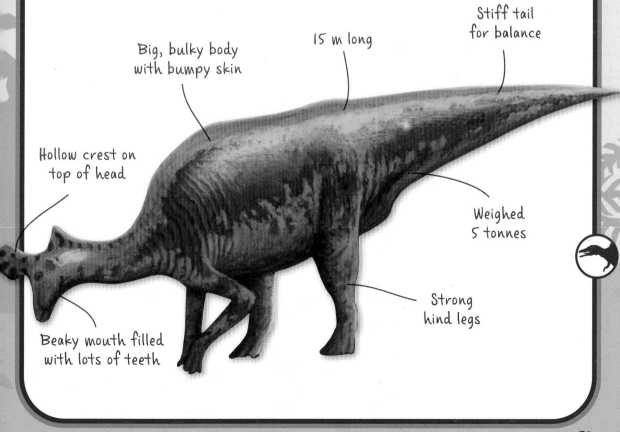

Big, bulky body with bumpy skin

15 m long

Stiff tail for balance

Hollow crest on top of head

Weighed 5 tonnes

Strong hind legs

Beaky mouth filled with lots of teeth

LEAELLYNASAURA

This small plant eater was named Lea Ellyn's Reptile after the young daughter of its discoverer. Its fossils come from the famous Dinosaur Cove coastal cliff site near Melbourne, Australia. *Leaellynasaura* had large eye sockets, and along with plant fossils from the site, this suggests that it may have lived in thick forest and so had big eyes to see in the gloom. It had a beak-like mouth for eating vegetation such as ferns, cycads and flowering plants, which were spreading around the world at the time.

SCALE

Australia used to be much colder than it is today, so Leaellynasaura may have hibernated in the cold season.

FACT FILE

Latin name
Leaellynasaura amicagraphica
Pronounced
lee-ell-in-uh-SAW-ruh
Group Ornithopod
Diet Herbivore
When it lived 120 mya

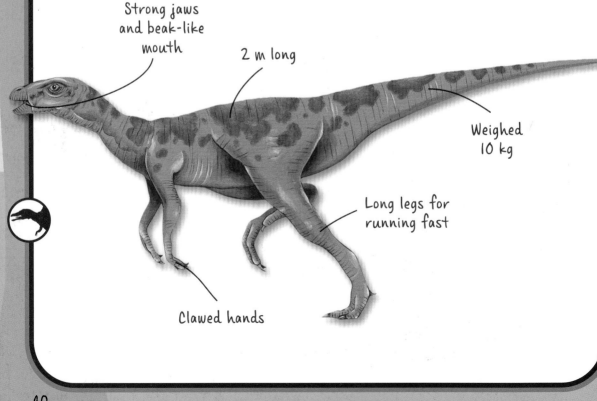

Strong jaws and beak-like mouth

2 m long

Weighed 10 kg

Long legs for running fast

Clawed hands

MAIASAURA

This large plant eater was a duckbilled dinosaur. In the 1970s, huge collections of *Maiasaura* skeletons of all ages were found in Montana, USA. This showed that these dinosaurs bred in groups called colonies, and each laid its eggs in a nest scooped out of earth. The teeth of the babies were worn from eating, yet their limb bones were not yet developed enough for walking. The parent dinosaur may have brought food to them in the nest, which is why the name *Maiasaura* means Good Mother Reptile.

SCALE

Maiasaura was the first dinosaur in space. A piece of bone and an eggshell were sent into space in 1985.

FACT FILE

Latin name
Maiasaura peeblesorum
Pronounced my-uh-SAW-ruh
Group Ornithopod
Diet Herbivore
When it lived 80 mya

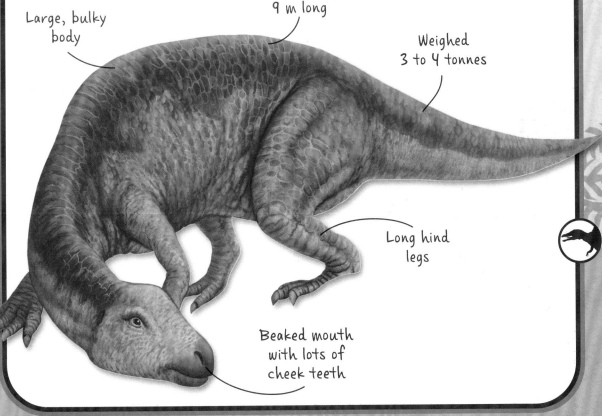

Large, bulky body

9 m long

Weighed 3 to 4 tonnes

Long hind legs

Beaked mouth with lots of cheek teeth

MUTTABURRASAURUS

A cousin of *Iguanodon*, *Muttaburrasaurus* had a bulge on its toothless, horned snout that reached from its nostrils to its eyes. This may have been used to make loud calling sounds. It probably moved on two legs, but may have been able to run on all four. To feed, it would stand on all four legs in order to reach low bushes or rear up on its back legs to reach higher trees. Like *Iguanodon*, *Muttaburrasaurus* had large thumb spikes.

SCALE

Large spikes on the hands of Muttaburrasaurus may have been used to stab predators or to pick up food.

FACT FILE

Latin name
Muttaburrasaurus langdoni

Pronounced
mut-a-burr-a-SAW-rus

Group Ornithopod

Diet Herbivore

When it lived 110 mya

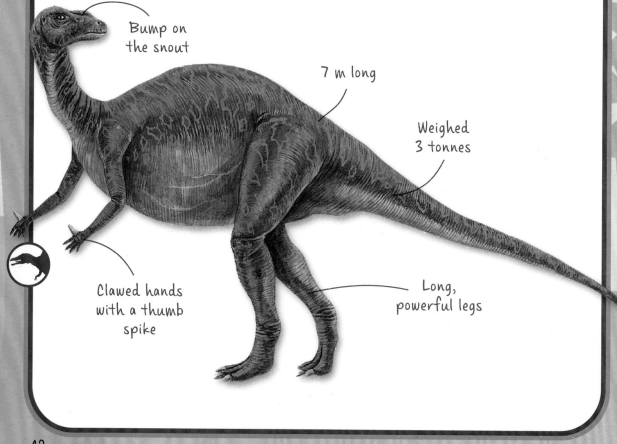

Bump on the snout

7 m long

Weighed 3 tonnes

Clawed hands with a thumb spike

Long, powerful legs

ORNITHOMIMUS

This dinosaur is thought to be omnivorous, eating both plants and small animals. Its mouth was shaped like a bird's beak and made out of a tough, strong, horny substance like human fingernails. It pecked at all kinds of food such as seeds, worms and bugs, but its head is thought to be too small to be able to hunt larger prey. The long arms with their clawed fingers could grasp food to eat. It was able to run fast to escape predators.

SCALE

FACT FILE

Latin name
Ornithomimus velox

Pronounced
or-NITH-o-MEE-mus

Group Theropod

Diet Omnivore

When it lived 77 mya

Ornithomimus could probably reach speeds of 70 km/h – the same speed as a modern-day ostrich.

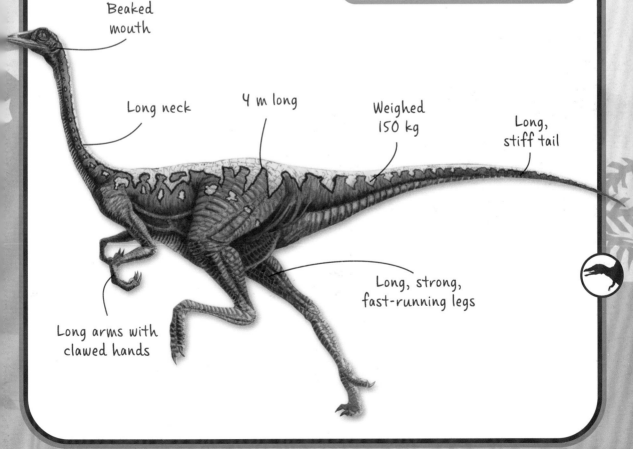

Beaked
mouth

Long neck

4 m long

Weighed
150 kg

Long,
stiff tail

Long arms with
clawed hands

Long, strong,
fast-running legs

OVIRAPTOR

The name *Oviraptor* means 'Egg Thief' as the first of its fossils were found lying among the broken eggs of another dinosaur. Instead of teeth, *Oviraptor* had a strong, curved beak, like that of a parrot or eagle, which was used to crack open eggs. On its forehead was a tall, rounded piece of bone, like a crest, that may have been to signify dominance in a group. *Oviraptor* fossils have been found in the Gobi Desert in Asia.

SCALE

FACT FILE

Latin name
Oviraptor philoceratops
Pronounced o-vee-RAP-tor
Group Theropod
Diet Omnivore
When it lived 83 mya

Oviraptor had two bony spikes inside its mouth that it may have used to crack eggs when it closed its jaws.

Head crest

2 m long

Weighed 30 kg

Parrot-like mouth

Long, powerful legs for running

Long arms and claws for grabbing prey

PACHYCEPHALOSAURUS

This strange-looking dinosaur belonged to the 'bonehead' group. It had a large, bony dome on top of its skull, which protected its skull in possible headbutting contests. However, scientists now think that this is unlikely as the adult skulls probably didn't stand up to such heavy use. Instead, these dinosaurs may have butted each other, or enemies, on the shoulder or flank.

Pachycephalosaurus had five fingers on each hand – a primitive feature for a dinosaur that appeared so late.

FACT FILE

Latin name *Pachycephalosaurus wyomingensis*

Pronounced pack-ee-KEF-ah-low-saw-rus

Group Pachycephalosaur

Diet Herbivore

When it lived 76 mya

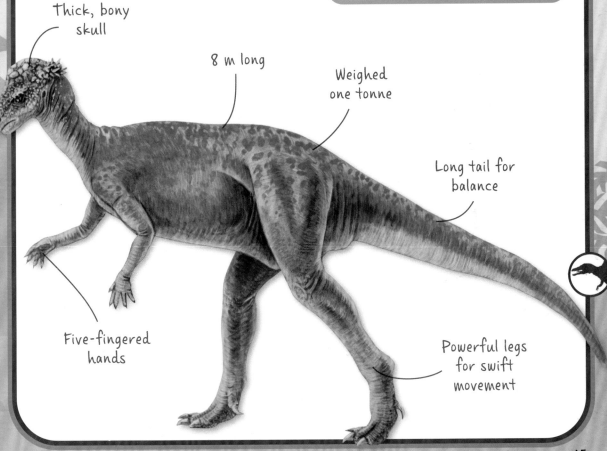

Thick, bony skull

8 m long

Weighed one tonne

Long tail for balance

Five-fingered hands

Powerful legs for swift movement

PARASAUROLOPHUS

Of the many kinds of duckbilled dinosaur, the longest head crest belonged to *Parasaurolophus*. This strange structure stuck up and back from the skull for almost 2 m. It was not solid bone, but contained two air tubes that led from the nostrils, passed up inside the front of the crest, looped over at the top and then passed down again, on the way to the lungs. This dinosaur may have been able to blow air through its crest to make a low honking sound, like a trombone or foghorn.

SCALE

When scientists first discovered Parasaurolophus, they thought its head crest was a giant snorkel.

FACT FILE

Latin name
Parasaurolophus walkeri

Pronounced
pa-ra-saw-ROL-off-us

Group Ornithopod

Diet Herbivore

When it lived 75 mya

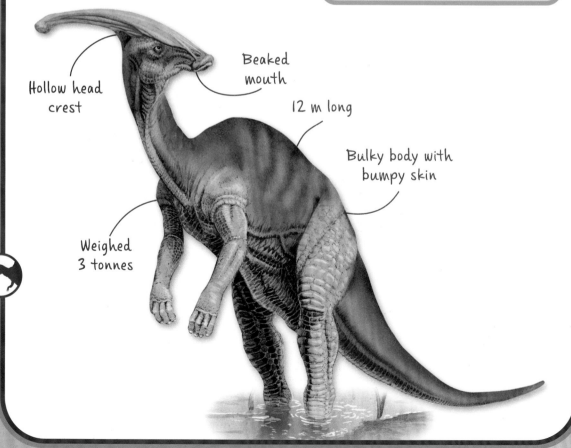

Hollow head crest

Beaked mouth

12 m long

Bulky body with bumpy skin

Weighed 3 tonnes

POLACANTHUS

One of the early armoured dinosaurs, *Polacanthus* was a huge, lumbering herbivore. The formation of its protective spikes is not clear, but they may have jutted out from the shoulders. Although covered in bony plates and spikes, its soft underbelly made it vulnerable to attack. It is not certain whether *Polacanthus* had a tail club for swinging at enemies. Its fossils have been found in southern England and at various sites on mainland Europe.

SCALE

A primitive ankylosaur, the first fossils of Polacanthus were found on a cliff face on the Isle of Wight in England.

FACT FILE

Latin name *Polacanthus foxii*
Pronounced pol-a-KAN-thus
Group Ankylosaur
Diet Herbivore
When it lived 125 mya

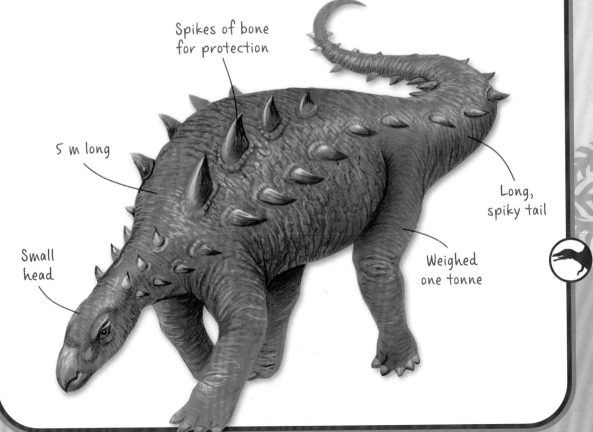

Spikes of bone
for protection

5 m long

Small
head

Long,
spiky tail

Weighed
one tonne

PROTOCERATOPS

This dinosaur lived in the region that is now the Gobi Desert in Asia. *Protoceratops* is an ancestor of the ceratopsian (horn-faced) dinosaurs and resembles the more famous member, *Triceratops*, but it was actually much smaller. Its neck frill was also small and plain compared to those of the later ceratopsians. *Protoceratops* had a tough beak used for cropping vegetation and two small horn-like bumps on the sides of its face.

SCALE

A fossilized Protoceratops has been found locked in battle with a Velociraptor, fighting to the death.

FACT FILE

Latin name
Protoceratops andrewsi
Pronounced pro-toe-SAIR-o-tops
Group Ceratopsian
Diet Herbivore
When it lived 82 mya

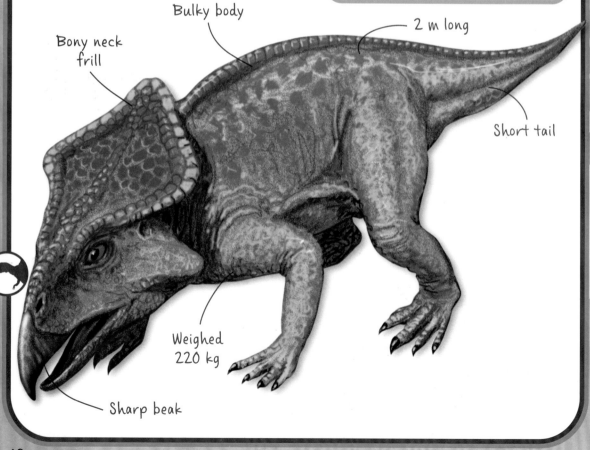

Bulky body

Bony neck frill

2 m long

Short tail

Weighed 220 kg

Sharp beak

PSITTACOSAURUS

An early type of horned dinosaur (ceratopsian), *Psittacosaurus* had not developed the nose horn or neck frill. In 2004 an amazing discovery in China showed the remains of an adult *Psittacosaurus*, a small parrot-beaked plant eater, surrounded by more than 30 young. This suggests the adult was caring for the young when they all died in a sudden disaster.

SCALE

FACT FILE

Latin name
Psittacosaurus mongolensis
Pronounced sit-ACK-oh-SAW-rus
Group Ceratopsian
Diet Herbivore
When it lived 120 mya

Fossil evidence shows that when first hatched, the young Psittacosaurus were hardly bigger than a human hand.

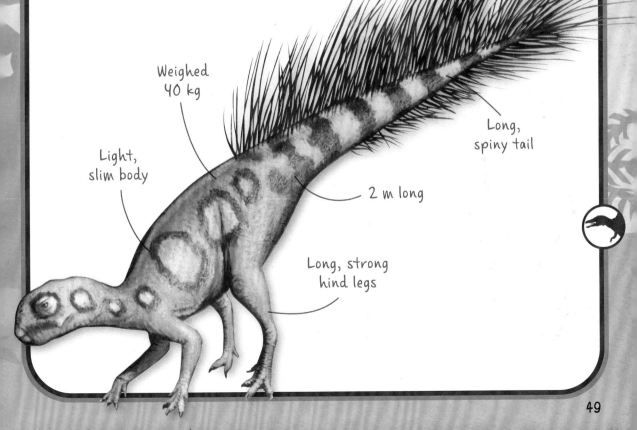

Weighed
40 kg

Light,
slim body

Long,
spiny tail

2 m long

Long, strong
hind legs

SALTASAURUS

One of the last great sauropods, *Saltasaurus* is unusual in this group as it had protective bony lumps and plates on its skin. These ranged from the size of a human hand down to the size of a shirt button. It also had a short neck for a sauropod, a muscular tail and a low stocky body. *Saltasaurus* may have been able to rear up onto its back legs to eat leaves from the tallest trees.

SCALE

Some of the bony plates on the body of Saltasaurus may have had sharp spikes sticking out from them.

FACT FILE

Latin name
Saltasaurus loricatus

Pronounced salt-ah-SAW-rus

Group Sauropod

Diet Herbivore

When it lived 70 mya

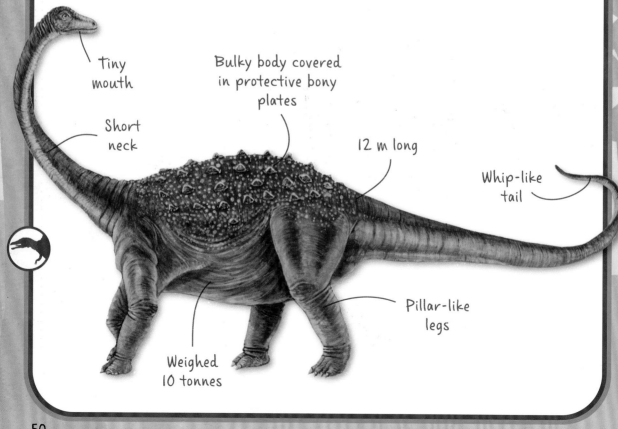

Tiny mouth

Short neck

Bulky body covered in protective bony plates

12 m long

Whip-like tail

Pillar-like legs

Weighed 10 tonnes

SPINOSAURUS

A large meat eater, *Spinosaurus* had a long, crocodile-like head, similar to that of *Baryonyx*. Its teeth were slim and sharp, suggesting that it scavenged for food on rotting carcasses. It has given its name to a group of theropod dinosaurs, the spinosaurs. *Spinosaurus* also had a distinctive 'sail' on its back, formed of skin held up by long, bony rods. The sail was almost 2 m tall and may have been a way of controlling body temperature, or to attract a mate at breeding time.

SCALE

The teeth of Spinosaurus were as sharp as knives, but they were straight – not curved like other dinosaur teeth.

FACT FILE

Latin name
Spinosaurus aegyptiacus
Pronounced spin-o-SAW-rus
Group Theropod
Diet Carnivore
When it lived 98 mya

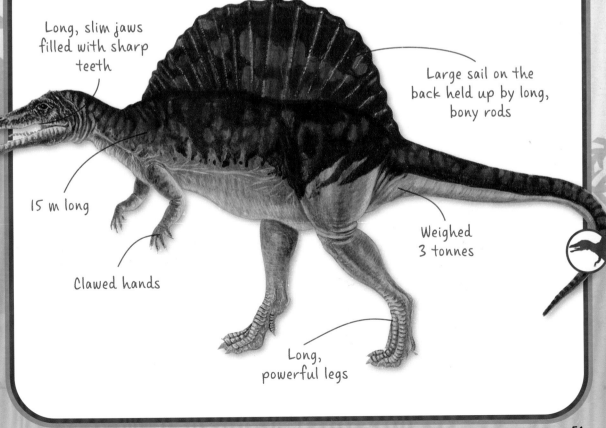

Long, slim jaws filled with sharp teeth

Large sail on the back held up by long, bony rods

15 m long

Clawed hands

Weighed 3 tonnes

Long, powerful legs

TRICERATOPS

The biggest of the horned dinosaurs, or ceratopsians, *Triceratops* was no easy victim for predators such as Tyrannosaurus rex. Its eyebrow horns were almost one metre long and its wide, bony neck frill was larger than a dining table. *Triceratops* would have charged with twice the bulk and power of today's rhinoceros. But most of the time it probably snipped off vegetation with its sharp parrot-like beak, and munched this food with its many sharp-ridged cheek teeth.

SCALE

Triceratops was twice the size of a modern rhinoceros. It also lived in herds, which protected it from enemies.

FACT FILE

Latin name *Triceratops horridus*
Pronounced try-SAIR-o-tops
Group Ceratopsian
Diet Herbivore
When it lived 65 mya

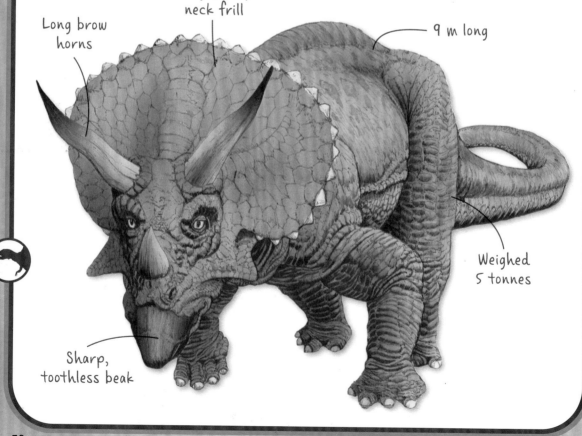

Large, bony neck frill

Long brow horns

9 m long

Weighed 5 tonnes

Sharp, toothless beak

TROODON

This big-brained dinosaur was a slender, lightweight hunter of small lizards, birds, mammals and other small prey. Its fossils show that its eyes were large, and from the shape of the brain cavity inside the skull, it had keen senses of sight, hearing and smell. *Troodon* would have stood chest-high to a person and could probably move at speed. Its name means 'Wounding Tooth', which refers to its saw-edged teeth.

SCALE

Troodon had the largest brain, compared to body size, of any dinosaur.

FACT FILE

Latin name *Troodon formosus*
Pronounced true-don
Group Theropod
Diet Carnivore
When it lived 76 mya

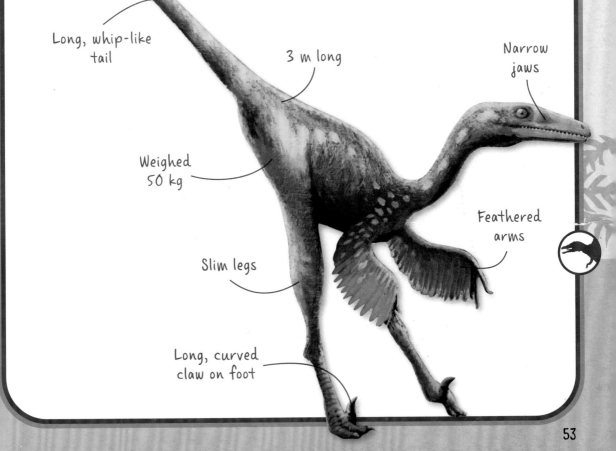

Long, whip-like tail

3 m long

Narrow jaws

Weighed 50 kg

Feathered arms

Slim legs

Long, curved claw on foot

TYRANNOSAURUS REX

Famous for being the biggest hunting animal ever to walk the land, *Tyrannosaurus rex* has lost this record to *Giganotosaurus*. However, *Tyrannosaurus rex* remains the dinosaur we love to fear. Its mouth opened so wide that it could have easily swallowed a ten-year-old child. This great predator lived in North America and was one of the last dinosaurs to appear.

SCALE

The teeth of Tyrannosaurus were 15 to 25 cm in length and were powerful enough to crunch through bone.

FACT FILE

Latin name *Tyrannosaurus rex*
Pronounced tie-Ran-o-SAW-rus
Group Theropod
Diet Carnivore
When it lived 67 mya

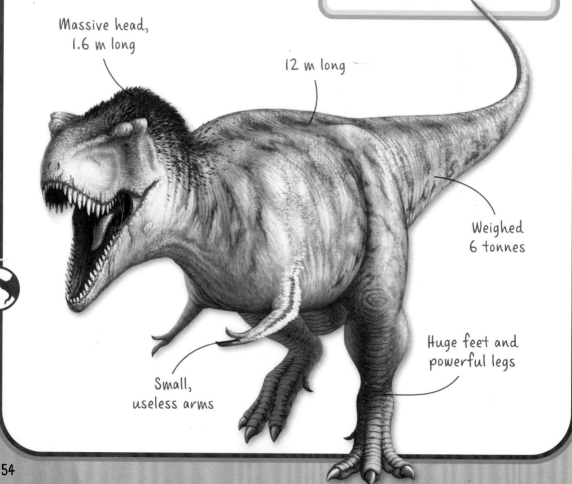

Massive head, 1.6 m long

12 m long

Weighed 6 tonnes

Huge feet and powerful legs

Small, useless arms

VELOCIRAPTOR

This dinosaur was a powerful, agile meat eater. With a super-sharp claw on each foot, it was capable of cutting metre-long gashes into its prey. It lived in what is now the dry scrub and desert of Mongolia, Central Asia. *Velociraptor* probably ran fast and could leap great distances on its powerful hind legs.

SCALE

Although it was a fierce meat eater, Velociraptor was no bigger than a modern-day Great Dane dog.

FACT FILE

Latin name
Velociraptor mongoliensis
Pronounced ve-LOSS-ih-RAP-tor
Group Theropod
Diet Carnivore
When it lived 85 mya

Sharp, curved teeth

2 m long

Long tail for balance

Weighed 20 kg

Long legs for leaping onto victims

Huge, sharp claw for tearing at prey

GLOSSARY

Camouflaged When an animal is shaped, coloured or patterned to blend in with its surroundings.

Carnivore An animal that eats only or mostly meat.

Ceratopsian The family of dinosaurs that was characterized by having horns on their heads.

Dinosaur A group of reptiles characterized by having legs that were tucked directly underneath their bodies.

Dinosauria The large group of reptiles that dinosaurs belonged to.

Evolve The gradual change in which animals and plants adapt to survive the changing world around them.

Fossil A part of an animal or plant that has been preserved, usually in rock.

Herbivore An animal that eats only or mostly plants.

Ornithischian One of two main types of dinosaur. Ornithischians had hips shaped like those of modern-day birds. All ornithischian dinosaurs were plant eaters.

Pachycephalosaur The family of dinosaurs that had very thick skull bones.

Palaeontologist A scientist who studies prehistoric animals and plants.

Predator A meat-eating animal that hunts and kills other creatures for food.

Prehistoric A time in history before anything was written down.

Prosauropod The family of dinosaurs that could walk on two or four legs and ate plants. They lived before the sauropods.

Reptile A group of animals characterized by having scaly skin and are cold blooded.

Saurischian One of two main types of dinosaur. Saurischians had hips shaped like those of modern lizards.

Sauropod The family of plant-eating dinosaurs that walked on four legs and reached enormous sizes.

Scavenge To feed on meat from the body of an animal that has died from disease or other natural causes.

Stegosaur The family of plant-eating dinosaurs that had plates or spikes growing along their backs.

Theropod A general term for two-legged meat-eating dinosaurs.

Vertebrae The bones that are joined together to form the backbone.

Warm-blooded An animal that is able to generate its own body heat, rather than absorbing heat from its surroundings.